When God's Word
Does Not Make Sense
To Your Natural Senses...OBEY

Ms S Scroppins.

Be blessed &
be a "doer" of
His word.

Handle

July 2010

When God's Word
Does Not Make Sense
To Your Natural Senses...OBEY

BUNMI AKINDEBE

Outskirts Press, Inc.
Denver, Colorado

Acknowledgements

Foremost, I am grateful to God for the inspiration to write this book.

To Mrs. Jumoke Akinola who typed the initial manuscript, I say a big thank you.

All members of Salem Gospel Mission Int'l Bronx Assembly, I say thank you for all what God has used you for in one way or the other in my life, ministry, and in the work of the Lord. God bless you all.

Pastor Stephen Akinwekomi, you are loved too. Thank you for been my pastor in my early Christian walk.

To all my sisters-Ronke, Bukky, Mowa and my only brother Seye, you are loved from my heart.

Finally to the love of my life, my darling wife Deaconess Dupe Akindebe and our children, I say thank you for your understanding and supporting me all the way.

God be with you all.

Foreword

The author of this book is a minister of God with passion for God's word. In a simple Biblical narrative form, he has taken up one of the subjects of Biblical theology, which is obedience to Divine Revelation when it sounds foolish to the natural sense. For a book of this like to come out at a time like this is a welcome development in this age of doubt and disobedience to God and his word.

When God speaks through His word, it is man's responsibility to respond with obedience.

The whole Bible carries the language of obedience. In the Old and New Testaments the word "Sama" conveys the meaning of both "to hear" and "to obey." Abraham was blessed because he heard and obeyed the Lord's voice. (Genesis 22: 18)

Jesus call to discipleship involves the "doing" ethics. According to Paul, obedience is one of the constituent parts of faith. Christ stands as the model of obedience. Philip. 2: 5-8

As you prayerfully read this book, you cannot but be challenged to see the essence of obedience and faith as the means to get the best from God.

This is my prayer for all who have contact with this book.

Bishop (Dr) J.O. Fatunwase
Moderator & Apostolic Father
Salem Gospel Mission Int'l
Ibadan.
Oyo State, Nigeria.

Dedication

This book is dedicated to the loving memory of my late father, Joel Adegbemisoye Akindebe, a lover of education who sacrificed so much for my education and for all my siblings.

About the Author

Bunmi Akindebe is the Pastor of Salem Gospel Mission Int'l, Bronx New York, USA. He is an in-depth teacher of the Word of God, preaching holiness in line with Hebrews 12:14 "…holiness without which no man shall see the Lord."

Bunmi Akindebe, a graduate of University of Ibadan, Nigeria is married to beautiful Dupe Akindebe (Nee Oyewola) and blessed with three anointed and gifted children.

Preface

It is not what you know that is important. What you do with what you know it's what is important. As you pick this book to read, maybe in your car, in your friend's house, in a bookstore, in an office table, sitting or standing, or in an elevator, anywhere it may be, whether you are a believer and follower of Christ or not, my prayer is that you will feel the Divine Presence of God in your life at that moment.

What is important as you decide to pick up this book to read is what you will do with the information inside this book. Are you going to read it and be a doer of the word, or not? Hear ye the word of God in the book of James 1:21-25

"Wherefore lay apart all filthiness and superfluity of naughtiness, and receive with meekness the engrafted word, which is able to save your souls.

But be ye doers of the word, and not hearers only, deceiving your own selves.

For if any be a hearer of the word, and not a doer, he is like unto a man beholding his natural face in a glass:

For he beholdeth himself, and goeth his way, and straightaway forgetteth what manner of man he was.

But whoso looketh into the perfect law of liberty, and continueth therein, he being not a forgetful hearer, but a doer of the work, this man shall be blessed in his deed."

May you be doer of the word of God, that's my prayer for you.

Contents

Introduction

The word of God is the final authority in every situation and every circumstance. You might have gone various ways to seek help that hasn't worked, or hasn't produced an answer or intended solution. And in some cases when there seems to be a help (which I personally call false help), it doesn't last. The word of God clearly states, if you receive help from Egypt (i.e. not from God) **"…when the Lord shall stretch out his hand, both he that helpeth shall fall, and he that is holpen shall fall down, and they all shall fail together." (Isaiah 31: 3).**

I have searched through the scriptures and found out that obedience is all we need to make it to heaven and to live a prosperous and productive life on earth, and this is the problem with Satan (Lucifer), for he could not obey. And ever since, Satan has been working in the hearts of people, causing them not to obey the word of God.

God in His word clearly states that our thoughts and ways are not His thoughts and ways. So when God's way of help, deliverance, solution, or answer doesn't make sense to us, then remember what the scripture says in Isaiah 55:8 **"For my thoughts are not your thoughts, neither are your ways my ways, saith the Lord."**

People of the world say, "Seeing is believing." This can be translated as walking by sight. To us children of God, "Believing is seeing" translated as walking by faith – even when everything is looking like and suggesting failure.

May the good Lord richly bless you as you read this book, and make you be a doer of the word, whether it makes sense or not to your natural senses. **"But be ye doers of the word, and not hearers only, deceiving your own selves."** (James 1:22).

Let me pause here a little bit and say authoritatively that there is a consequence for disobedience. A typical example for us is in the book of 1 Corinthians 10:1-11

"Moreover, brethren, I would not that ye should be ignorant, how that all our fathers were under the cloud, and all passed through the sea, and they were all baptized unto Moses in the cloud and in the sea; and did all eat the same spiritual meat, and did all drink the same spiritual drink; for they drank of that spiritual rock that followed them, and that rock was Christ. But with many of them God was not well pleased, for they were overthrown in the wilderness. Now these things were our examples, to the intent we should not lust after evil things, as they also lusted. Neither be ye idolaters, as were some of them, as it is written. The people sat down to eat and drinks, and rose up to play. Neither let us commit fornications, as some of them committed, and fell in one day three and twenty thousand. Neither let us tempt Christ, as some of them also

tempted, and were destroyed of serpents. Neither murmur ye, as some of them also murmured, and were destroyed of the destroyer. Now all these things happened unto them for ensamples and they were written for our admonition, upon whom the ends of the world are come."

In terms of application of the scripture quoted, what we need to ponder is verse 5: "but with many of them God was not well pleased." Why was God not well pleased? The answer is because they failed to obey God's word. God was pleased only with Joshua and Caleb, and only they were allowed to enter the land of Canaan. The book of Numbers 14:22 – 24, says **"…because all those men which have seen my glory, and my miracles, which I did in Egypt and in the wilderness and have tempted me now these ten times, and have not hearkened to my voice, surely they shall not see the land which I swore to their fathers, neither shall any of them that provoked me see it. But my servant Caleb, because he has another spirit with him and hath followed me fully, him will I bring into the land where into he went and his seed shall possess it."**

In Numbers 14: 28-30 God further proclaims, **"Say unto them, as truly as I live, saith the Lord, as ye have spoken in mine ears, so will I do to you. Your carcasses shall fall in this wilderness and all that were numbered of you, according to your whole number, from twenty years old and upward, which have murmured against me. Doubtless ye shall not come unto the land, concerning which I swore to make you dwell therein, save Caleb the son of Jephunneh, and Joshua the son of Nun."**

Pray for the spirit of Caleb and Joshua to be in you. That is the spirit of obedience and trust in God, even when everything around you in your natural senses suggests failure.

You could see from the scriptures, therefore, that disobedience led to the deaths of many who left the land of Egypt, while obedience saved the lives of two (Caleb and Joshua).

Looking at this story further in terms of analysis, and physical evidence and circumstances, every indication looks like the Israelites cannot overcome the inhabitants of Canaan.

Numbers 13: 31-33 **"But the men that went up with him said, we be not able to go up against the people; for they are stronger than we, and they brought up an evil report of the land which they had searched unto the children of Israel, saying, the land, through we have gone to search it, it is a land that eateth up the inhabitants thereof; and all the people that we saw in it are men of a great stature. And there we saw the giants, the sons of Anak, which come of the giants; and we were in our own sight as grasshoppers, and so we were in their sight."**

- they are stronger
- they eateth up the inhabitants thereof
- they are men of great stature
- they saw giants, the sons of Anak
- they saw themselves (Israelites) as grasshoppers

But whose report would you believe the report of God or of mere men? Isaiah 53:1 **"Who hath believed our report?"**

the report of men as spoken by the 10 spies "....we be not able to up against the people, for they are stronger than we." (Numbers 13: 31)

But the report of God says: **"Hear, O Israel, thou art to pass over Jordan this day, to go on to possess nations greater and mightier than thyself, cities great and fenced up to heaven. A people great and tall, the children of the Anakims, whom thou knowest and of whom thou hast heard say, who can stand before the children of Anak. Understand therefore this day, that the Lord thy God is he which goeth over before thee, as a consuming foe he shall destroy them, and he shall bring them down before thy face so shall thou drive them out and destroy them quickly, as the Lord hath said unto thee."** (Deuteronomy 9: 1-3). Believe and obey God's report. One interesting thing to point out to readers of this story is that what the spies saw in Numbers 13 is exactly what God describes in Deut. 9 : 1- 3, only they did not believe the report of the Lord. The spies were using their natural senses. Brethren, when what you see or read doesn't make sense to your natural senses, just obey.

But despite all these things that suggest failure using natural senses, Caleb said they should go forward. Why? Because God said so, and because of Caleb's obedience, he was blessed and was given an inheritance (Hebron) because **"....he wholly followed the Lord God of Israel."** (Joshua 14: 14)

If Noah had acted on his natural senses, the boat wouldn't have been built. Who knows if people around him in those days asked Noah the following questions?

Question:	Noah, what are you doing?
Noah:	I am building an ark of gopher wood.
Question:	You are building what!!!
Noah:	An ark.
Question:	Why are you building this ark?
Noah:	God told me to build an ark.
Question:	For what purpose?
Noah:	There is going to be a flood that would consume all flesh because of their wickedness.
Question:	Noah are you crazy? Where could you see rain on the horizon?

If Noah had acted on his natural senses by considering these questions, it probably would have been a different story. But thank God, **"thus did Noah, according to all that God commanded him, so did he."** (Genesis 6: 22)

Let us consider our father Abraham when he God said to him **"….get thee out of thy country, and from thy father's house, unto a land that I will shew thee."** (Gen. 12:1). The Bible records that Abraham departed, but before the departure, consider the following likely questions that the people might have asked Abraham:

Question:	Abraham, where are you going?
Abraham:	I am going to a place but don't know the place right now.
Question:	How can you be going to a place you don't know, or who told you to go to this place?
Abraham:	My God, the God of Israel.
Question:	Are you crazy?
Abraham:	No.

Had he been acting on his natural senses and these scenario questions and answers, Abraham wouldn't have departed. But thank God that **"Abraham departed, as the Lord had spoken unto him."** (Genesis 12:4)

WHAT IS OBEDIENCE?

Simply put, according to the New Webster's Dictionary and Thesaurus of the English Language, obedience is defined as "submission of one's own will to the will, expressed or otherwise, of another to an impersonal embodiment of authority."

Stop right there and think of what the Lord Jesus Christ said in Gethsemane on Mount Olives in Luke 22:42 **"Father, if thou be willing, remove this cup from me: nevertheless not my will, but thine be done."**

You can see here that it is not the will of Jesus Christ (in humanity), but God's will. So my brethren in the Lord, to make it to heaven, to receive God's promises and blessings, we need and we have to submit our will, and say like Jesus Christ, not my will, but thine be done O Lord.

Let us look at and examine the following:

1. Obedience to God
2. Obedience to Government
3. Obedience to Masters
4. Obedience to Husbands
5. Obedience to Teachers
6. Obedience to Parents

OBEDIENCE TO GOD

This is the most supreme, because if you surrender your will and obey GOD first, it will not be difficult for you to obey the others listed above. Why? Jesus Christ said in John 14: 23 **"If a man love me, he will keep my words and my father will love him, and we will come unto him and make our abode with him."** What are the words of our Lord Jesus Christ? The words are that we should love one another, for God is love (I John 4: 7), and that he should **"love his brother also"** (I John 4: 21). So it is clear that if we love GOD and obey his words, (his commandments), then it will be easier to love others, (whether husband, teachers, parents, masters, etc).

Obedience to GOD is the <u>duty</u> required of every child of GOD. In Deuteronomy 26: 16, God said through Moses **"This day the Lord thy GOD hath commanded thee to do these statutes and judgments, thou shall therefore keep and do them with all thine heart and with all thy soul."** You can see it is our duty to obey -- remember, not your will, but the will of GOD.

Obedience to parents is a commandment of God that does not leave a choice. Ephesians 6: 1-3 **"Children obey your parents in the Lord, for this is right. Honor thy father and mother, which is the first commandment with promise. That it may be well with thee, and thou mayest live long on the earth."** The Bible says for this is right, because your parents in the Lord will give you advice and instructions in the Lord to help prepare you for Godly success in life. That is why God said in Proverbs 1: 8-9 **"My son, hear the instruction of thy father and forsake not the law of thy mother, for they shall be as ornament of grace onto thy head and chains around thy neck."** God also said in Proverbs 6: 20-23 **"My son, keep thy father's commandment and forsake not the law of thy mother. Bind them continually upon their heart and tie them around thy neck. When thou goest, it shall lead thee, when thou sleepest, it shall keep thee, and when thou awakest, it shall talk with thee. For the commandment is a lamp, and the law is light, and reproofs of instruction are the way of life."** All these scriptures above have their root in the Ten Commandments the Lord gave to Moses at Mount Sinai in Exodus 20: 12 **"Honor thy father and thy mother, that thy days may be long upon the land which the Lord thy God giveth thee."** Summarily, this is not your will -- whether you like it or not, it is a commandment. Remember the saying of Jesus Christ: if you love me, you will obey my words.

God further enjoins us in the book of Colossians 3: 20 **"Children, obey your parents in all things, for this is well pleasing unto the Lord."** Godly parents will give and train their children the same manner God teaches. However, when there is a conflict between a parent's instructions and God's instructions, of course, we should obey God rather than men. Acts 5: 29 **"Then Peter and the other apostles answered and said, we ought to obey GOD rather than men."** Obedience to our teachers too is of the Lord (Proverbs 5: 12-13).

Obedience to husbands too is of the Lord as written in the book of Col. 3: 18 **"Wives, submit yourselves unto your own husbands, as it is fit in the Lord."** Also, Titus 2:5 **"To be discreet, chaste, keepers at home, good and obedient to their own husbands, that the word of GOD be not blasphemed."**

We are also to be obedient to our masters as found in Ephesians 6: 5 **"Servants, be obedient to them that are your masters according to the flesh, with fear and trembling in singleness of your heart, as unto the Lord."** *(Also read Colossians 3: 22; Titus 2: 9; I Peter 2: 18).*

Lastly, God made provision to obey the government as found in Titus 3: 1 **"Put them in mind to be subject to principalities and powers, to obey magistrates, to be ready to do every good work."** Here it is talking about our civil leaders'and institutions of government. I Peter 2:13-14 **said "Submit yourselves to every ordinance of man for the Lord's sake: whether it be to king, as supreme, or unto governors, as unto them that are sent by him for the punishment of evil doers, and for the praise of them that do well."**

This is not a matter of choice, but an obligation for us Christians. This is something that Christians should do willingly, joyfully, without any compulsion, for the Lord's sake. It is because of this obedience to government that we pay taxes like everyone, obey traffic regulations like everyone, etc.

In conclusion, the fear of God is to be the chief concern of man as recorded in the book of Ecclesiastes 12:13 **"Let us hear the conclusion of the whole matter: fear God, and keep his commandments: for this is the whole duty of man."**

1

Story of Quails
(Numbers 11:1-24)

"And when the people complained, it displeased the Lord: and the Lord heard it, and his anger was kindled; and the fire of the Lord burnt among them, and consumed them that were in the uttermost parts of the camp. And the people cried unto Moses; and when Moses prayed unto the Lord, the fire was quenched. And he called the name of the place Tabera: because the fire of the Lord burnt among them. And the mixed multitude that was among them fell a lusting: and the children of Israel also wept again, and said, who shall give us flesh to eat? We remember the fish, which we did eat in Egypt freely; the cucumbers, and the melons, and the leeks, and the onions, and the garlick: But now our soul is dried away: there is nothing at all, beside this manna, before our eyes. And the manna was as coriander seed, and the color thereof as the color of bdellium. And the people went about, and gathered it, and ground it in the mills, or beat it in a mortar, and baked it in pans, and made cakes of it: and the taste of it was as the taste of fresh oil. And when the dew fell upon in the night, the manna fell upon it. Then Moses heard the people weep through their families, every man in the door of his tent: and the anger of the Lord was kindled greatly: Moses also was displeased. And Moses said unto the Lord, wherefore hast thou afflicted me thy servant? And wherefore have I not found favor in thy sight, that thou layest the burden of all this people upon me? Have I conceived all this people? Have I begotten them, that thou shouldest say unto me, carry them in thy bosom, as a nursing father beareth the suckling child, unto the land which thou swarest unto their fathers? Whence should I have flesh to give unto all these people? For they weep unto me, saying Give us flesh that we may eat. I am not able to bear all this people alone, because it is too heavy for me. And if thou deal thus with me, kill me, I pray thee, out of hand, if I have found favor in thy sight, and let me not see wretchedness. And the Lord said unto Moses, gather unto me seventy men of the elders of Israel, whom thou knowest to be the elders of the people, and officers over them, and bring them unto the tabernacle of the congregation, that they may stand there with thee. And I will come down and talk with thee there, and I will take of the spirit which is upon thee, and will put it upon them; and they shall bear the burden of the people with thee, that thou bear it not thyself alone. And say thou unto the people, Sanctify yourself against tomorrow, and ye shall eat flesh: for ye have wept in the ears of the Lord, saying, who shall give us flesh to eat? for it was well with us in Egypt: therefore the Lord will give you flesh, and ye shall eat it. Ye shall not eat one day, nor two days, nor five days, neither ten days, nor twenty days; but even a whole month, until it come out at your nostrils, and it be loathsome unto you: because that ye have despised the Lord which is among you, and have wept before him, saying, Why came we forth out of Egypt? And Moses said, the people, among whom I am, are six hundred thousand footmen, and thou hast said, I will give them flesh, that they may eat a whole month. Shall the flocks and the herds be slain for them, to suffice them? Or shall all the fish of the sea be gathered together for them, to suffice them? And the Lord said unto Moses, Is the Lord's hand waxed short? Thou shall see now whether my word shall come to pass unto thee or not. And Moses went out, and told the people the words of the Lord, and gathered the seventy men of the elders of the people, and set them round about the tabernacle."

There was a time when the Israelites were fed up with eating manna from heaven, and they complained. God was not pleased with their murmuring. In His infinite mercies, He decided to give them quail and told His servant Moses, **"And say thou unto the people, sanctify yourselves against tomorrow, and ye shall eat flesh: for ye have wept in the ears of the Lord, saying, who shall give us flesh to eat? For it was well with us in Egypt: therefore the Lord will give you flesh and ye shall eat."** (Numbers 11:18)

Moses responded to GOD using his natural senses saying, **"…the people, among whom I am, are six hundred thousand footmen; and thou hast said, I will give them flesh, that they may eat a whole month. Shall the flocks and the herds be slain for them to suffice them? Or shall all the fish of the sea be gathered together for them to suffice them."** (Numbers 11: 21-22). Moses was referred to as the meekest man on the surface of the earth, but when God tells him that He is going to feed the whole nation of Israel, Moses operating by his natural senses, saw this as an impossible task; Moses was applying *"seeing is believing" formula*

But the Bible clearly stated that his children should use "Believing is seeing," i.e. walking by faith. God responded to Moses **"And the Lord said unto Moses, is the Lord's hand waxed short? Thou shall see now whether my word shall come to pass unto thee or not."** (Numbers 11: 23). Also **"…for with God nothing shall be impossible."** Luke 1:37

WHEN GOD'S WORD DOES NOT MAKE SENSE...

This is where I pray this book will be a blessing unto you by believing God's word, whether it makes senses to you or not. Moses now believed and obeyed, by doing what the Lord commanded him to do (vs. 24). It was after his (Moses) part was fulfilled, that GOD came and stepped into the situation and brought the quails as promised. **"And there went forth a wind from the Lord, and brought quails from the sea, and let them fall by the camp, as it were a day's journey on this side, and as it were a day's journey on the other side, round about the camp, and as it were two cubits high upon the face of the earth."** Numbers 11:31.

The application of this today is that in your situation (whatever it is), there is a way, there is a solution, there is an answer, there is a promise in His Holy word -- search the scriptures and look for the promises for your situation, appropriate them, act on them, believe on them (and of course it will not make sense to your natural senses), and then the Lord will come down unto the situation and fulfill His own part.

When you are believing and acting on the word of GOD, people might make fun of you and your action that looks foolish and stupid, but this is the point at which you need to act and stand firm. **"For the preaching of the cross is to them that perish foolishness; but unto us which are saved it is power of GOD."** (1 Corinthians 1:18).

He that hath an ear let him hear what the spirit saith unto the churches.

2

Story of an Axe Head
(2 Kings 6:1-7)

"And the sons of the prophets said unto Elisha, behold now, the place where we dwell with thee is too strait for us. Let us go, we pray thee, unto Jordan, and take thence every man a beam, and let us make us a place there, where we may dwell. And he answered, Go ye. And one said, be content, I pray thee, and go with thy servants. And he answered, I will go. So he went with them. And when they came to Jordan, they cut down wood. But as one was felling a beam, the axe head fell into the water: and he cried, and said, Alas, master! For it was borrowed. And the man of God said, where fell it? And he shewed him the place. And he cut down a stick, and cast it in thither; and the iron did swim. Therefore said he, Take it up to thee, and he put out his hand, and took it."

This is a story/miracle of GOD at His best. What is an axe? It is a tool made of handle fitted with a steel/iron cutting head, used for cutting down trees or chopping, splitting etc. It is usually of considerable weight that the law of gravity is always associated with this tool if it is in water. It must sink, it must go down.

WHEN GOD'S WORD DOES NOT MAKE SENSE...

Here God demonstrated that His answers to this borrowed axe would not make sense to scientists, the physicists, the engineers, and the learned. There is power of God in this situation. The axe head in the first place was borrowed. Where it does not make sense to human senses is the fact that after the man of GOD (Prophet Elisha) asked his servant where the axe fell, the Bible says he cut down a stick. To do what? To cast (throw) it to the area/spot. And what happened? The Bible recorded it that the iron did swim.

Can you imagine your child coming home from school calling your attention, telling you, asking you to observe what he/she is about to do. First he/she asked you (borrowed a quarter 25 cents) from you, (remember the axe head was borrowed,) next he/she took a bowl filled with water placed in the living room and dropped the 25 cents into the bowl and ran outside and looked for a stick, probably from a tree on your property, and came back with the stick. You would ask him/her what he/she was up to. As a loving parent who wants their children to exploit will however ask at this stage what kind of stupid game or idea he/she is up to.

Your child responded that he/she is going to make the 25 cents float using the stick in his hand. You will probably pay him/her no attention. There the stick was cast into the bowl and the 25 cents did float and swim. This would definitely draw your attention. You would probably want to look at the stick to see whether there is a hidden magnet to draw the 25 cents, or what was it that made the money float.

This is what the story in 2 Kings 6: 1-7 is all about -- the power of GOD comes down when you act and obey the voice of GOD. Elisha cut a stick, and God's power followed to bring a lost object.

STORY OF AN AXE HEAD

Cutting the stick doesn't make sense to solve gravitational problems; casting it into the sea doesn't make sense either. But supernaturally something (the power of God) that we cannot see took place between the floating stick and the drowned axe head.

Please obey and act on God's word and leave the rest to GOD for HIS accomplishment, HIS glory, and HIS Majesty; and let the blessings be yours.

3

The Story of Simon Peter and Fishing
(Luke 5:1-11)

"And it came to pass, that, as the people pressed upon him to hear the word of God, he stood by the lake of Gennesaret, and saw two ships standing by the lake; but the fishermen were gone out of them, and were washing their nets. And he entered into one of the ships, which was Simon's and prayed him that he would thrust out a little from the land. And he sat down, and taught the people out of the ship. Now when he had left speaking, he said unto Simon, launch out into the deep, and let down your nets for a draught. And Simon answering said unto him, Master, we have toiled all the night, and have taken nothing: nevertheless at thy word I will let down the net. And when they had this done, they inclosed a great multitude of fishes: and their nets break. And they beckon unto their partners, which were in the other ship, that they should come and help them. And they came, and they filled both the ships, so that they began to sink. When Simon Peter saw it, he fell down at Jesus knees, saying, depart from me, for I am a sinful man, O Lord. For he was astonished, and all that were with him, at the draught of the fishes which they had taken. And so was also James, and John, the sons of Zebedee, which were partners with Simon. And Jesus said unto Simon, Fear not; from henceforth thou shall catch men. And when they had brought their ships to land, they forsook all, and followed him."

This is a classic example of what obedience can do in our lives, if we just obey the master (Jesus Christ), even when all circumstances suggest failure.

In this story Simon Peter has gone out to fish at the best time to catch fish, at night, and he did not catch anything. So Jesus Christ coming into the scene and telling him now at daytime when the probability of catching fish is zero, could make Peter or anyone with his/her natural senses to say no, and that you are out of your mind. Or he might even have said: haven't you read in the Bible (if he/she is a Christian) in Psalm 104:20-23 that **"Thou makest darkness and it is night, wherein all the beasts of the forest do creep forth. The young lions roar after their prey, and seek their meat from GOD. The sun ariseth, they gather themselves together, and lay down in their dens. Man goeth forth unto his work and to his labor until the evening."**

Arguments could be made in this Simon Peter scenario that at night the best time to catch fish, there was nothing and "the sun ariseth makes the probability impossible.

In general, some fish like the Wels Catfish (Latin name – Silurus Glanis) are nocturnal feeders and become active at dusk. Surprise is their method of attack -- they use the cover of darkness to get close to their prey. During the day, they lay up in cover, if there is a mud on the bottom this will be used to settle into.

THE STORY OF SIMON PETER AND FISHING

Other interesting facts to observe in this story are:

1. The fishermen (one of them Peter) were washing their nets. The point is that after each period of fishing, the normal and the traditional thing to do is for fishermen to wash their nets. They remove debris, mend them if need be, stretch them in preparation for use again, maintain boats and supplies, supervise crews, etc. All these take a lot of long, tiring hours after landing ashore. This is enough reason for Peter to tell the master (Jesus Christ) NO at Jesus request to **"let down your nets for a draught"** Luke 5: 4.

2. In Luke 5:3 **"And he entered into one of the ships, which was Simon's and prayed him that he would thrust out a little from the land. And he sat down, and taught the people out of the ship. Jesus went to the ship and taught the people out of the ship."** Jesus went to the ship and taught the people out of the ship before Jesus told Peter to let down for a draught. The duration of the teaching time was not recorded in the bible, but the fact that Jesus Christ taught for some time could indicate to the natural senses that day was breaking, or this was daytime, because as it is recorded in Luke 5: 1 **"…as the people pressed upon him to hear the word of GOD… ."** So the probability of catching fish at this time of the day, using our natural senses, is zero.

Now let us look at what obedience did in the life of Peter and what it could do in your life. Luke 5:5 **"And Simon answering said unto him, master, we have toiled all the night, and have taken nothing: nevertheless at thy word I will let down the net."** You see, brethren; Simon here is not operating with his natural senses any more. He is not operating from his own will any more. He is not operating by his power any more. His own power has produced nothing. He is not operating by his own intuition any more. He is not operating by natural circumstances any more. It was at this point of obedience to the word of the master and letting down the net into the sea again that **"they inclosed a great multitude of fishes and their nets brake."** Luke 5:6.

In terms of application in your life today, have you been toiling all night and day like Simon and produced nothing? Have you allowed or are your being ruled by your natural senses instead of God's word? Are you saying let my will be done, instead of God's will in your life? The answer to break through in your life, brethren, is to be obedient to the word of God, even when it doesn't make sense to your natural senses (like it didn't make sense to Simon). Remember **"we walk by faith and not by sight"** (2 Cor 5:7).

4

The Story of Naaman's Leprosy and Healing
(2 Kings 5: 1-19)

"Now Naaman, captain of the host of the king of Syria, was a great man with his master, and honorable, because by him the LORD had given deliverance unto Syria: he was also a mighty man in valor, *but he was* a leper. And the Syrians had gone out by companies, and had brought away captive out of the land of Israel a little maid; and she waited on Naaman's wife. And she said unto her mistress, would God my lord *were* with the prophet that *is* in Samaria! for he would recover him of his leprosy. And *one* went in, and told his lord, saying, Thus and thus said the maid that *is* of the land of Israel. And the king of Syria said, Go to, go, and I will send a letter unto the king of Israel. And he departed, and took with him ten talents of silver, and six thousand *pieces* of gold, and ten changes of raiment. And he brought the letter to the king of Israel, saying, Now when this letter is come unto thee, behold, I have *therewith* sent Naaman my servant to thee, that thou mayest recover him of his leprosy. And it came to pass, when the king of Israel had read the letter, that he rent his clothes, and said, *Am* I God, to kill and to make alive, that this man doth send unto me to recover a man of his leprosy? wherefore consider, I pray you, and see how he seeketh a quarrel against me. And it was *so*, when Elisha the man of God had heard that the king of Israel had rent his clothes, that he sent to the king, saying, Wherefore hast thou rent thy clothes? let him come now to me, and he shall know that there is a prophet in Israel. So Naaman came with his horses and with his chariot, and stood at the door of the house of Elisha. And Elisha sent a messenger unto him, saying, Go and wash in Jordan seven times, and thy flesh shall come again to thee, and thou shalt be clean. But Naaman was wroth, and went away, and said, Behold, I thought, He will surely come out to me, and stand, and call on the name of the LORD his God, and strike his hand over the place, and recover the leper. *Are* not Abana and Pharpar, rivers of Damascus, better than all the waters of Israel? may I not wash in them, and be clean? So he turned and went away in a rage.

And his servants came near, and spake unto him, and said, My father, *if* the prophet had bid thee *do some* great thing, wouldest thou not have done *it*? how much rather then, when he saith to thee, Wash, and be clean? Then went he down, and dipped himself seven times in Jordan, according to the saying of the man of God: and his flesh came again like unto the flesh of a little child, and he was clean. And he returned to the man of God, he and all his company, and came, and stood before him: and he said, Behold, now I know that *there is* no God in all the earth, but in Israel: now therefore, I pray thee, take a blessing of thy servant. But he said, *As* the LORD liveth, before whom I stand, I will receive none. And he urged him to take *it*; but he refused. And Naaman said, Shall there not then, I pray thee, be given to thy servant two mules' burden of earth? for thy servant will henceforth offer neither burnt offering nor sacrifice unto other gods, but unto the LORD. In this thing the LORD pardon thy servant, *that* when my master goeth into the house of Rimmon to worship there, and he leanest on my hand, and I bow myself in the house of Rimmon: when I bow down myself in the house of Rimmon, the LORD pardon thy servant in this thing. And he said unto him, Go in peace. So he departed from him a little way."

The story of Naaman is that of a man who is operating by his natural perception. And to be honest, there is nothing wrong with walking by your natural senses if you are not a believer, but after having an encounter with the master, we should let old things pass away. Proverbs 3: 5-8 says **"trust in the Lord with all thine heart, and lean not unto thine own understanding, in all thy ways acknowledge him, and he shall direct your paths. Be not wise in their own eyes, fear the Lord, and depart from evil. It shall be health to thy navel, and marrow to thy bones."**

Naaman was a captain of the host of the king of Syria. He was a successful man in every sense, except with the phrase **"but he was a leper."** (2 Kings 5:1) This was a dreadful disease at this time which called for ostracism.

From this background you could understand the healing that this man needed. When the Lord used a small girl (little maid) to tell Naaman to go and see a prophet in Samaria **"for he would recover him of his leprosy" (vs. 3).** Naaman went to the prophet with his own understanding of how the healing would take place.

WHEN GOD'S WORD DOES NOT MAKE SENSE...

The man of God in question, the prophet Elisha, prescribed unto him (Naaman) saying, **"go and wash in Jordan seven times, and thy flesh shall come again to thee, and thou shall be clean,"** (2Kings 5:10). To Naaman, this does not make sense -- what kind of type of healing is this? The issue of bathing seven times is not understandable to Naaman, and he questions the choice of the River Jordan rather than the river Abana or river Pharpar in Damascus (vs.12). Historically, the Abana River in downtown Damascus, Syria as known today is the Barada River. Naaman considered this river and the Pharpar River of his native land superior to the Jordan River in Israel. That's why he made those statements that "**are not Abana and Pharpar rivers of Damascus, better than all the waters of Israel? May I not wash in them and be clean? So he turned and went away in rage." (vs.12)** God's prescription of healing seems to cause disbelief, anger, and humiliation to a captain in the Syrian army. The point here is one of obedience.

Let us talk a little bit about the issue of seven times. In the time of Moses, God had given instructions about the rites and sacrifices in the cleansing of a leper as recorded in Leviticus 14:1-32. **"And the LORD spake unto Moses, saying, This shall be the law of the leper in the day of his cleansing: He shall be brought unto the priest: And the priest shall go forth out of the camp; and the priest shall look, and, behold, if the plague of leprosy be healed in the leper; Then shall the priest command to take for him that is to be cleansed two birds alive and clean, and cedar wood, and scarlet, and hyssop: And the priest shall command that one of the birds be killed in an earthen vessel over running water: As for the living bird, he shall take it, and the cedar wood, and the scarlet, and the hyssop, and shall dip them and the** living bird in the blood of the bird that was killed over the running water: And he shall sprinkle upon him that is to be cleansed from the leprosy seven times, and shall pronounce him clean, and shall let the living bird loose into the open field. And he that is to be cleansed shall wash his clothes, and shave off all his hair, and wash himself in water, that he may be clean: and after that he shall come into the camp, and shall tarry abroad out of his tent seven days. But it shall be on the seventh day that he shall shave all his hair off his head and his beard and his eyebrows, even all his hair he shall shave off: and he shall wash his clothes, also he shall wash his flesh in water, and he shall be clean. And on the eighth day he shall take two he-lambs without blemish, and one ewe lamb of the first year without blemish, and three tenth deals of fine flour for a meat offering, mingled with oil, and one log of oil. And the priest that maketh him clean shall present the man that is to be made clean, and those things, before the LORD, at the door of the tabernacle of the congregation: And the priest shall take one he-lamb, and offer him for a trespass offering, and the log of oil, and wave them for a wave offering before the LORD: And he shall slay the lamb in the place where he shall kill the sin offering and the burnt offering, in the holy place: for as the sin offering is the priest's, so is the trespass offering: it is most holy: And the priest shall take some of the blood of the trespass offering, and the priest shall put it upon the tip of the right ear of him that is to be cleansed, and upon the thumb of his right hand, and upon the great toe of his right foot: And the priest shall take some of the log of oil, and pour it into the palm of his own left hand: And the priest shall dip his right finger in the oil that is in his left hand, and shall sprinkle of the oil with his finger seven times before the LORD: And of the rest of the oil that is in his hand shall the priest put upon the tip of the right ear of him that is to be cleansed, and upon the thumb of his right hand, and upon the great toe of his right foot, upon the blood of the trespass offering: And the remnant of the oil that is in the priest's hand he shall pour upon the head of him that is to be cleansed: and the priest shall make an atonement for him before the LORD. And the priest shall offer the sin offering, and make an atonement for him that is to be cleansed from his uncleanness; and afterward he shall kill the burnt offering: And the priest shall offer the burnt offering and the meat offering upon the altar: and the priest shall make an atonement for him, and he shall be clean. And if he be poor, and cannot get so much; then he shall take one lamb for a trespass offering to be waved, to make an atonement for him, and one tenth deal of fine flour mingled with oil for a meat offering, and a log of oil; And two turtledoves, or two young pigeons, such as he is able to get; and the one shall be a sin offering, and the other a burnt offering. And he shall bring them on the eighth day for his cleansing unto the priest, unto the door of the tabernacle of the congregation, before the LORD. And the priest shall take the lamb of the trespass offering, and the log of oil, and the priest shall wave them for a wave offering before the LORD: And he shall kill the lamb of the trespass offering, and the priest shall take some of the blood of the trespass offering, and put it upon the tip of the right ear of him that is to be cleansed, and upon the thumb of his right hand, and upon the great toe of his right foot: And the priest shall pour of the oil into the palm of his own left hand: And the priest shall sprinkle with his right finger some of the oil that is in his left hand seven times before the LORD: And the priest shall put of the oil that is in his hand upon the tip of the right ear of him that is to be cleansed, and upon the thumb of his right hand, and upon the great toe of his right foot, upon the place of the blood of the trespass offering: And the rest of the oil that is in the priest's hand he shall put upon the head of him that is to be cleansed, to make an atonement for him before the LORD. And he shall offer the one of the turtledoves, or of the young pigeons, such as he can get; Even such as he is able to get, the one for a sin offering, and the other for a burnt offering, with the meat offering: and the priest shall make an atonement for him that is to be cleansed before the LORD. This is the law of him in whom is the plague of leprosy, whose hand is not able to get that which pertaineth to his cleansing."

One of the instructions is to sprinkle blood collected from one of the birds killed on the leper seven times, after which he shall wash himself in water. Probably Naaman knew he was going to be told to wash in water, but why not in the Abana River or Pharpar River? That's why he made that statement.

Now going back to the Prophet Elisha's prescription to Naaman, it is according to the standard of God. Go wash in river Jordan seven times. A leprous man must wash himself in water on the first day, and on the seventh day (Lev. 14: 8-9). God said in Isaiah 55: 8-11 **"for my thoughts are not your thoughts, rather are your ways my ways, saith the Lord."** Until we allow the thoughts and ways of God to overcome our thoughts and ways, (which is obedience) nothing will get accomplished in one's life.

WHEN GOD'S WORD DOES NOT MAKE SENSE...

This is what happened to Naaman -- he came to the prophet with his own thoughts and ways of healing, instead of obeying the word of God through Prophet Elisha; he went back in rage and did not obey the word of God. The Bible recorded that he went back in rage, and his servants persuaded him to obey and do what the Prophet of GOD asked him to do, after which he went down and did exactly as he was told.

What I want us to look carefully here is that Naaman was still carrying his leprosy with him between the period that he went away in rage and the time his servants came and spoke unto him. The Bible did not record the time period between going away in rage and the time his servants spoke to him. This could be minutes, hours, weeks, or months. The lesson is that his problem did not go away during this period. Most of the children of God today have heard from the living God and have not obeyed, and so the situation or problems in their lives haven't changed.

It was after Naaman put his own thoughts and ways aside, stopped leaning on his own understanding, and obeyed and did exactly as he was told, that he received his healing.

Your situation will change for good the moment you heed God's word. Your healing will come immediately when you heed the word of God. Your circumstances will change for the better when you allow the word of God in your life.

Proverb 4:20-22 says **"My son, attend to my words, incline thine ear unto my sayings. Let them not depart from thine eyes: keep them in the midst of thine heart for they are life unto those that find them, and health to all their flesh."** It was after Naaman *"attended"* to the words of God spoken by Prophet Elisha that he found health to his flesh. Wonderful.

Even though Naaman was cured of leprosy by God's grace, and there was nothing meritorious about Naaman dipping in the Jordan River, Naaman would not have been cured without dipping seven times in the Jordan River. He was only cleansed after dipping seven times. Not one, two, three, four, five, or six times, but only after seven times. He would not have been cleansed dipping in the Abana or Pharpar Rivers there at Damascus, only in the Jordan River. He would not have been cleansed by being sprinkled with the waters of the Jordan River. He had to dip under the water. In like manner, even though we are saved by grace and not by works, we cannot be saved without obedience. Jesus said, ***"Not every one that saith unto me, Lord, Lord, shall enter into the kingdom of heaven; but he that doeth the will of my Father which is in heaven."*** (Matthew 7:21). James wrote, ***"Wherefore lay apart all filthiness and superfluity of naughtiness, and receive with meekness the engrafted word, which is able to save your souls. But be ye doers of the word, and not hearers only, deceiving your own selves. For if any be a hearer of the word, and not a doer, he is like unto a man beholding his natural face in a glass: For he beholdeth himself, and goeth his way, and straightway forgetteth what manner of man he was. But whoso looketh into the perfect law of liberty, and continueth therein, he being not a forgetful hearer, but a doer of the work, this man shall be blessed in his deed."*** (James 1:21-25). Jesus likened the person that hears the word but doesn't obey to a foolish man (Matthew 7:26, 27). We cannot leave out or substitute for baptism. Baptism is a burial: ***"Therefore we are buried with him by baptism into death:***

that like as Christ was raised up from the dead by the glory of the Father, even so we also should walk in newness of life." (Romans 6:4). You cannot substitute sprinkling for baptism and expect God to accept it as obedience.

<u>We see how presumption nearly cost Naaman salvation from his leprosy</u>. When Naaman was told by Elisha's servant to go dip seven times in the Jordan River, he was angry and the first words recorded out of his mouth were, *"Behold, I thought..."* (II Kings 5:11). People are like Naaman today. They presume that as long as they are sincere in what they think, what they feel, what they believe to be right, that God will save them. We can no more be saved from our sins by our own volition than Naaman was cleansed of his leprosy. **Naaman's pride nearly cost him his salvation.** When Naaman found that his salvation from his disease depended on him dipping seven times in the Jordan River he was angry. He made excuses why he would not obey this command, like, **"Are not Abana and Pharpar, rivers of Damascus, better than all the waters of Israel? may I not wash in them, and be clean?"** (II Kings 5:12). But Naaman's servants knew the real reason; it was his pride. After all, Naaman was a warrior, a man of great valor, a man who went above and beyond the call of duty. He had put his life on the line for king and country many a time. That is the reason why the king of Syria trusted Naaman with his very life. Dipping in the River Jordan would not bring him any honor or any fame. His servants recognized that it was pride that kept him from doing as Elisha had instructed and asked him, **"My father, if the prophet had bid thee do some great thing, wouldest thou not have done it? how much rather then, when he saith to thee, Wash, and be clean?"** (II Kings 5:13). Naaman finally realized that his

pride was keeping him from being free of this horrible, crippling disease and went down to Israel and dipped seven times in the River Jordan. Many today will not obey the Gospel of Christ because it will not bring them honor or fame. They want to be saved, but by their own merit. That was the way the Pharisee was in Jesus's story in Luke 18:10-14, but Jesus said that **"every one that exalteth himself shall be abased"** (Luke 18:14). We are saved by the Grace of God, not by our own works (Titus 3:4-7). We are not saved because of our works, but because of the works that Jesus the Christ did on the cross of Calvary (Romans 5:5-11). It is our duty to God to obey, but it does not merit our salvation (Luke 17:7-10). We are not saved through meritorious works. This doctrine would be a stumbling block to the Jews and foolishness to the Gentiles (I Corinthians 1:23). Only those who humble themselves and obey God will be saved (James 4:6; Matthew 21:28-32).

What Have We Learnt?

Naaman believed unto obedience and went and dipped seven times in the River Jordan and was cleansed from his leprosy. Likewise, we must believe unto obedience, turning away from sins and being baptized. Naaman could not be cured of his leprosy by the method he thought was right. He was only cured of his leprosy after he had done all that he had been commanded to do. We cannot be saved by what we think or feel in our heart is right, no matter how sincere we are. We can be saved only according to the plan God has laid out for us in His word. Naaman was a mighty man of valor. God had used Naaman in punishing the Northern Kingdom of Israel. Yet all his mighty deeds could not save him from his terrible disease. It was the grace of God that cleansed him of his leprosy. We are not saved by meritorious works. We do not -- cannot -- earn salvation. We are saved by the work that Jesus the Christ did on the cross on Golgotha.

In summary, when God's way or idea or words do not make sense to us, just like the word did not make sense to Naaman, just obey. For this is where and when the healing and breakthrough will happen in one's life. Be blessed.

5

The Story of the Widow's Oil
(2 Kings 4: 1-7)

"Now there cried a certain woman of the wives of the sons of the prophets unto Elisha, saying, Thy servant my husband is dead; and thou knowest that thy servant did fear the LORD: and the creditor is come to take unto him my two sons to be bondmen. And Elisha said unto her, What shall I do for thee? tell me, what hast thou in the house? And she said, Thine handmaid hath not any thing in the house, save a pot of oil. Then he said, go, borrow thee vessels abroad of all thy neighbors, *even* empty vessels; borrow not a few. And when thou art come in, thou shalt shut the door upon thee and upon thy sons, and shalt pour out into all those vessels, and thou shalt set aside that which is full. So she went from him, and shut the door upon her and upon her sons, who brought *the vessels* to her; and she poured out. And it came to pass, when the vessels were full, that she said unto her son, Bring me yet a vessel. And he said unto her, *there is* not a vessel more. And the oil stayed. Then she came and told the man of God. And he said, Go, sell the oil, and pay thy debt, and live thou and thy children of the rest."

WHEN GOD'S WORD DOES NOT MAKE SENSE...

This story of the widow's oil as written in the Bible, I believe, by wisdom can be looked, digested, and meditated upon in various ways, and in whichever way it is looked at, the name of the Lord will still be glorified.

It could be looked at from:

- The aspect of God's concern for the poor and underprivileged
- The aspect of obedience of the widow

This is a woman who was in debt and went to the prophet of God for help by telling prophet Elisha of how bad the debt situation was, for **"the creditor is come to take unto him my two sons to be bondmen"** (2Kings 4:1). This in itself is a good step from the woman, for she went to look for help from God through the Prophet. God said in Isaiah 31:1 **"woe to them that go down to Egypt for help, and stay on horses, and trust in chariots, because they are many, and in horsemen, because they are very strong, but they look not unto the Holy one of Israel, neither seek the Lord."** So whatever is the problem you are facing, whether it is physical, spiritual, emotional, or financial (like the widow), make sure you seek the Lord for help. That's a good start and foundation.

The Prophet of God gave an answer by asking her if she had anything in the house and the widow's response was that she had a pot of oil. The answer from the Prophet of God to the widow was **"go borrow thee vessels abroad of all thy neighbors, even empty vessels, borrow not a few. And when thou art come in, thou shalt shut the door upon thee and upon thy sons, and shalt pour unto all those vessels, and thou shall set aside that which is full (vs.4),"**

THE STORY OF THE WIDOW'S OIL

Then, in verse 7, **"... he said, go sell the oil, and pay thy debts, and live thou and thy children of the rest."**

You see, this widow has a choice to believe or to not believe the prophet of God. Here we are talking about debt, the other party is talking about borrowing empty vessels, about oil, about pouring it unto the empty vessels not knowing what is going to happen next. Using our natural instinct, the prescribed solution above does not make any sense to resolve the situation at hand.

Remember the word of God says in Heb 3:12 **"Take heed, brethren, lest there be in any of you an evil heart of unbelief, in departing from the living GOD."** It is the believing GOD through his servant (Prophet Elisha) that delivered this widow from debt.

You want to get out of debt. Act on the word of God by obeying His word. Proverbs 11: 24-25 **says "There is that scattereth, and yet increaseth: and there is that withholdeth more than is meet, but it tendeth to poverty. The liberal soul shall be made fat: and he that watereth shall be watered also himself."**

To natural senses, it doesn't add up. One is scattering and yet increaseth, one withholds more than is meet, but tendeth to poverty. The widow did not withhold the little oil left with her and that's where the blessings came from.

It is the obedience of the widow to God's word that set her free from debt. Obey the word of GOD. You will be wonderfully blessed and be set free from debt too in the matchless name of Jesus (Amen).

6

The Story of a Man Born Blind Receiving Sight
(John 9: 1-41)

"And as *Jesus* passed by, he saw a man which was blind from *his* birth. And his disciples asked him, saying, Master, who did sin, this man, or his parents, that he was born blind? Jesus answered, neither hath this man sinned, nor his parents: but that the works of God should be made manifest in him. I must work the works of him that sent me, while it is day: the night cometh, when no man can work. As long as I am in the world, I am the light of the world. When he had thus spoken, he spat on the ground, and made clay of the spittle, and he anointed the eyes of the blind man with the clay, And said unto him, Go, wash in the pool of Siloam, (which is by interpretation, Sent). He went his way therefore, and washed, and came seeing. The neighbors therefore, and they which before had seen him that he was blind, said, Is not this he that sat and begged? Some said, This is he: others *said*, He is like him: *but* he said, I am *he*. Therefore said they unto him, How were thine eyes opened? He answered and said, A man that is called Jesus made clay, and anointed mine eyes, and said unto me, Go to the pool of Siloam, and wash: and I went and washed, and I received sight. Then said they unto him, Where is he? He said, I know not. They brought to the Pharisees him that aforetime was blind. And it was the Sabbath day when Jesus made the clay, and opened his eyes. Then again the Pharisees also asked him how he had received his sight. He said unto them, He put clay upon mine eyes, and I washed, and do see. Therefore said some of the Pharisees, This man is not of God, because he keepeth not the Sabbath day. Others said, How can a man that is a sinner do such miracles? And there was a division among them. They say unto the blind man again, What sayest thou of him, that he hath opened thine eyes? He said, He is a prophet. But the Jews did not believe concerning him, that he had been blind, and received his sight, until they called the parents of him that had received his sight. And they asked them, saying, Is this your son, who ye say was born blind? how then doth he now see? His parents answered them and said, We know that this is our son, and that he was born blind: But by what means he now seeth, we know not; or who hath opened his eyes, we know not: he is of age; ask him: he shall speak for himself. These *words* spake his parents, because they feared the Jews: for the Jews had agreed already, that if any man did confess that he was Christ, he should be put out of the synagogue. Therefore said his parents, He is of age; ask him. Then again called they the man that was blind, and said unto him, Give God the praise: we know that this man is a sinner. He answered and said, Whether he be a sinner *or no*, I know not: one thing I know, that, whereas I was blind, now I see. Then said they to him again, What did he to thee? how opened he thine eyes? He answered them, I have told you already, and ye did not hear: wherefore would ye hear *it* again? will ye also be his disciples? Then they reviled him, and said, Thou art his disciple; but we are Moses' disciples.

THE STORY OF A MAN BORN BLIND RECEIVING SIGHT

We know that God spake unto Moses: *as for* this *fellow*, we know not from whence he is. The man answered and said unto them, Why herein is a marvelous thing that ye know not from whence he is, and *yet* he hath opened mine eyes. Now we know that God heareth not sinners: but if any man be a worshipper of God, and doeth his will, him he heareth. Since the world began was it not heard that any man opened the eyes of one that was born blind. If this man were not of God, he could do nothing. They answered and said unto him, Thou wast altogether born in sins, and dost thou teach us? And they cast him out. Jesus heard that they had cast him out; and when he had found him, he said unto him, Dost thou believe on the Son of God? He answered and said, Who is he, Lord that I might believe on him? And Jesus said unto him, Thou hast both seen him, and it is he that talketh with thee. And he said, Lord, I believe. And he worshipped him. And Jesus said, For judgment I am come into this world, that they which see not might see; and that they which see might be made blind. And *some* of the Pharisees which were with him heard these words, and said unto him, Are we blind also? Jesus said unto them, If ye were blind, ye should have no sin: but now ye say, We see; therefore your sin remaineth."

For us to grasp the importance of obedience in this story, we need to know the materials used in this miracle, we need to know the biblical meaning and understanding of what clay is, and what potter is. In the book of Isaiah 64: 8 **"But now, O Lord, thou art our father, we are the clay and thou our potter, and we are all the work of thy hand."** You and I in essence by this definition are the clay (including this man born blind), Jesus Christ our Lord the potter. We also need to know what clay is used for. Biblically, one has power over the other. The potter here (Jesus Christ) has power over the clay (the man born blind). The word of GOD clearly confirms this in Jeremiah 18:1-6 **"The word which came to Jeremiah from the Lord saying, arise and go down to the potter's house, and there I will cause thee to hear my words. Then I went down to the potter's house, and, behold, he wrought a work on the wheels. And the vessel that he made of clay was marred in the hand of the potter; so he made it again another vessel, as seemed good to the potter to make it. Then the word of the Lord came to me saying, O house of Israel, cannot I do with you as this potter? saith the Lord. Behold, as the clay is in the potter's hand, so are ye in my hand, O house of Israel."**

So we could see that the potter controls what he does with the clay. The Lord has sovereignty over the people of Judah, over your life, over my life, over the man born blind. "... as the clay is in the potter's hand, so are ye in my hand, O house of Israel.

With this background, one now should not be surprised that the potter (Jesus Christ our Lord) **"spat on the ground, and make a clay of the spittle and he anointed the eyes of the blind man with clay"** (John 9:6) because the man born blind was made of clay. When a potter makes a vessel from clay unto a particular shape, and if he decides to change the vessel into another shape, the potter will remodel the vessel into another shape using the same clay. Jesus Christ answered his disciples that the man was born blind not because of sin, but for the glory of GOD to be revealed. The potter created him (the blind man) that way and so when he (the potter) wanted to shape the blind man into another vessel (shape) the potter had to use the same clay. Glory be to God in the highest.

THE STORY OF A MAN BORN BLIND RECEIVING SIGHT

After all this, Jesus Christ said unto him, **"Go, wash in the pool of Siloam"** (John 9:7). The Bible says the blind man "went his way therefore, and washed, and came seeing" (John 9:7).

The Bible recorded it that the blind man did not query Jesus Christ, did not ask him what has saliva and clay had to do with this, or why the pool of Siloam, but went and obeyed as he was commanded, and came seeing. This demonstrates that effort is needed on our part to be able to realize and appropriate God's manifold blessings in our life. We could say confidently that we need to exercise faith also in all of God's promises for our life. This action and saying of our Lord Jesus Christ of mud, saliva, and washing in water does not make sense to one's natural senses. The walking of the blind man to the pool of Siloam is what the Bible says we should all do *"for we walk by faith, not by sight"* (2 Corinthians 5:7).

The obedience and faith of this man born blind are instruments of his healing. So brethren, let us obey our Lord Jesus Christ (the potter) in every situation, for he is the one that made us and knows our substance. The Psalmist in Psalm 139:15-16 **says "my substance was not hid from thee, when I was made in secret, and curiously wrought in the lowest part of the earth. Thine eyes did see my substance, yet being imperfect and in thy book all my members were written, which in continuance were fashioned, when as yet there was none of them."** This is to say that your life, my life, and all structure are all established by GOD. Obedience to his word is the key to your healing today.

7

The Story of the Fall of Jericho
(Joshua 5:13-6:1-27)

"And it came to pass, when Joshua was by Jericho, that he lifted up his eyes and looked, and, behold, there stood a man over against him with his sword drawn in his hand: and Joshua went unto him, and said unto him, *Art* thou for us, or for our adversaries? And he said, Nay; but *as* captain of the host of the LORD am I now come. And Joshua fell on his face to the earth, and did worship, and said unto him, What saith my lord unto his servant? And the captain of the LORD'S host said unto Joshua, Loose thy shoe from off thy foot; for the place whereon thou standest *is* holy. And Joshua did so. Now Jericho was straitly shut up because of the children of Israel: none went out, and none came in. And the LORD said unto Joshua, See, I have given into thine hand Jericho, and the king thereof, *and* the mighty men of valor. And ye shall compass the city, all *ye* men of war, *and* go round about the city once. Thus shalt thou do six days. And seven priests shall bear before the ark seven trumpets of rams' horns: and the seventh day ye shall compass the city seven times, and the priests shall blow with the trumpets. And it shall come to pass, that when they make a long *blast* with the ram's horn, *and* when ye hear the sound of the trumpet, all the people shall shout with a great shout; and the wall of the city shall fall down flat, and the people shall ascend up every man straight before him. And Joshua the son of Nun called the priests, and said unto them, Take up the ark of the covenant, and let seven priests bear seven trumpets of rams' horns before the ark of the LORD. And he said unto the people, Pass on, and compass the city, and let him that is armed pass on before the ark of the LORD. And it came to pass, when Joshua had spoken unto the people, that the seven priests bearing the seven trumpets of rams' horns passed on before the LORD, and blew with the trumpets: and the ark of the covenant of the LORD followed them. And the armed men went before the priests that blew with the trumpets, and the rereward came after the ark, *the priests* going on, and blowing with the trumpets. And Joshua had commanded the people, saying, Ye shall not shout, nor make any noise with your voice, neither shall *any* word proceed out of your mouth, until the day I bid you shout; then shall ye shout. So the ark of the LORD compassed the city, going about *it* once: and they came into the camp, and lodged in the camp. And Joshua rose early in the morning, and the priests took up the ark of the LORD. And seven priests bearing seven trumpets of rams' horns before the ark of the LORD went on continually, and blew with the trumpets: and the armed men went before them; but the rereward came after the ark of the LORD, *the priests* going on, and blowing with the trumpets. And the second day they compassed the city once, and returned into the camp: so they did six days. And it came to pass on the seventh day that they rose early about the dawning of the day, and compassed the city after the same manner seven times: only on that day they compassed the city seven times. And it came to pass at the seventh time, when the priests blew with the trumpets, Joshua said unto the people, Shout; for the LORD hath given you the city. And the city shall be accursed, *even* it, and all that *are* therein, to the LORD: only Rahab the harlot shall live, she and all that *are* with her in the house, because she hid the messengers that we sent. And ye, in any wise keep *yourselves* from the accursed thing, lest ye make *yourselves* accursed, when ye take of the accursed thing, and make the camp of Israel a curse, and trouble it. But all the silver, and gold, and vessels of brass and iron, *are* consecrated unto the LORD: they shall come into the treasury of the LORD. So the people shouted when *the priests* blew with the trumpets: and it came to pass, when the people heard the sound of the trumpet, and the people shouted with a great shout, that the wall fell down flat, so that the people went up into the city, every man straight before him, and they took the city. And they utterly destroyed all that *was* in the city, both man and woman, young and old, and ox, and sheep, and ass, with the edge of the sword. But Joshua had said unto the two men that had spied out the country, Go into the harlot's house, and bring out thence the woman, and all that she hath, as ye sware unto her. And the young men that were spies went in, and brought out Rahab, and her father, and her mother, and her brethren, and all that she had; and they brought out all her kindred, and left them without the camp of Israel. And they burnt the city with fire, and all that *was* therein: only the silver, and the gold, and the vessels of brass and of iron, they put into the treasury of the house of the LORD. And Joshua saved Rahab the harlot alive, and her father's household, and all that she had; and she dwelleth in Israel *even* unto this day; because she hid the messengers, which Joshua sent to spy out Jericho. And Joshua adjured *them* at that time, saying, Cursed *be* the man before the **LORD**, that riseth up and buildeth this city Jericho: he shall lay the foundation thereof in his firstborn, and in his youngest *son* shall he set up the gates of it. So the **LORD** was with Joshua; and his fame was *noised* throughout all the country."

May the good Lord richly bless you as you read this part of this book, may He give you wisdom, and may you be hearer and doer of His word (if you have not been before now) We need to understand the following things/ facts about Jericho.

By biblical facts, Jericho was one of the oldest cites of Palestine. Bible recorded it as the first Canaanite city destroyed, after the Israelites crossed river Jordan (read Joshua chapter 4). Jericho was surrounded by a wall (fence) Joshua 6: 5 **"..and the wall of the city shall fall down flat ..."**

With this understanding let us examine how this wall of Jericho fell down flat. It was by faith. Faith is obedience to God's word. Hebrews 11:30 says **"By faith, the walls of Jericho fell down, after they were encompassed about 7 days."** This is to say, the destruction of the city of Palestine was not by conventional means of war, but by unconventional means:

- Faith (obedience) that led to the desired result.
- 7 Trumpets of rams' horns.
- 7 priests bearing the ark.
- Encompassing the city for 7 days and blowing of trumpets.

The children of the Israelites defeated Jericho with this unconventional means of waging war. These were people who were just stepping into the first city of the Canaanites; these were the people who for forty years have depended on GOD for supernatural feeding until the Lord withdrew the manna and they started eating from the produce of the land of Canaan (Joshua 5:11-12). Now the Lord told these people to go and fight a war, the first war after crossing river Jordan with these unconventional means. To our natural senses, this does not make sense. The obedience of Joshua and the people following God's instruction to the letter (to detail) gave them victory.

- The ark circled the city (Joshua 6: 10-11)
- This they did continually (Joshua 6:13) to follow the instructions of the Lord
- Joshua commanded them to shout (Joshua 6: 16)
- And the people shouted when the priests blew the trumpets **"that the wall fell down flat"** (Joshua 6:20)

In summary, the wall of Jericho fell down flat because they obeyed the word of GOD by faith (Hebrew 11:30) not looking at the fact that this city was **"greater and mightier than thou"** (Deuteronomy 7:1). Please obey the word of GOD even when it does not make sense to your natural senses. Joshua obeyed and did not doubt GOD and did not query GOD about why the trumpets, why dancing, why shouting, but by obeying.

These were the unconventional means GOD told them to use to fight this war. These people already had been told by GOD in the book of Deuteronomy 7 that they (the Israelites) are going to **"cast out many nations before them, the Hittites, and the Girgashites, and the Amorites and the Canaanites, and the Perizzites and the Hivites and the Jebusites, seven nations**

greater and mightier than them" (Deuteronomy 7:1). But God did not specify the means of defeating them.

So how, using your natural senses, do you think they could fight these nations with this unconventional means of war? This is where the power of God comes in when we obey his word. We should draw our strength from the Lord. When we face situations in our lives, and we look at God's instructions and promises, we should draw our strength from the Lord -- not looking at the present situation and predicament, we should remember God and the displacement of His power and glory in previous situations in the past. God said to his people in Deuteronomy 7:17-18 **"if thou shalt say in thine heart, these nations are more than I, how can I dispossess them? Thou shalt not be afraid of them, but shalt well remember what the Lord thy God did unto Pharaoh and unto all Egypt".**

In conclusion, remember that our God is a covenant making and covenant keeping God. Psalm 89: 34 says **"my covenant will I not break, nor alter the thing that is gone out of my lips."** Numbers 23: 19 **says "God is not a man that he should lie; neither the son of man that he should repent: hath he said, and shall he not do it? or hath he spoken, and shall he not make it good?"** The book of 2 Corinthians 10: 4 **says "for the weapons of our warfare are not carnal, but mighty through God to the pulling down of strongholds."**

When Jehoshaphat was invaded by Moabites, the war was won by Jehoshaphat not by conventional warfare of gun and cutlass, etc., but by fasting, singing songs, and praises. Does this make sense to your natural senses? Read the whole chapter of 2 Chronicles 20.

THE STORY OF THE FALL OF JERICHO

"Thus said the Lord unto you, be not afraid nor dismayed by reason of this great multitude; for the battle is not yours, but God's. Tomorrow go ye down against them; behold they come up by the cliff of Ziz; and ye shall find them at the end of the brook, before the wilderness of Jeruel. Ye shall not need to fight in this battle: set yourself, stand ye still, and see the salvation of the Lord with you, O Judah and Jerusalem: fear not, nor be dismayed; tomorrow go out against them: for the Lord will be with you ... and when they began to sing and to praise, the Lord set ambushments against the children of Ammon, Moab and mount Seir, which were come against Judah; and they were smitten." (vs. 15-22)

If the Lord had spoken a word concerning a situation, you had better believe it and act on it. God is not a man that he should lie. Jehoshaphat believed and obeyed, and success and victory came out of the situation -- so shall victory be yours when you act on God's word like Jehoshaphat. Be blessed.

8

The Story of Changing Water to Wine (John 2: 1-11)

"And the third day there was a marriage in Cana of Galilee; and the mother of Jesus was there: And both Jesus was called, and his disciples, to the marriage. And when they wanted wine, the mother of Jesus saith unto him, They have no wine. Jesus saith unto her, Woman, what have I to do with thee? mine hour is not yet come. His mother saith unto the servants, Whatsoever he saith unto you, do it. And there were set there six waterpots of stone, after the manner of the purifying of the Jews, containing two or three firkins apiece. Jesus saith unto them, Fill the waterpots with water. And they filled them up to the brim. And he saith unto them, Draw out now, and bear unto the governor of the feast. And they bare it. When the ruler of the feast had tasted the water that was made wine, and knew not whence it was: (but the servants which drew the water knew;) the governor of the feast called the bridegroom,
  And saith unto him, Every man at the beginning doth set forth good wine; and when men have well drunk, then that which is worse: but thou hast kept the good wine until now. This beginning of miracles did Jesus in Cana of Galilee, and manifested forth his glory; and his disciples believed on him."

WHEN GOD'S WORD DOES NOT MAKE SENSE...

There are many ways of looking at this story. It can be considered as:

- First miracle of our Lord Jesus Christ
- The significance of wedding as the will of GOD (in Genesis) confirmed by the presence of our Lord Jesus Christ in this marriage ceremony
- Obedience of the servants

Jesus was at a wedding where the wine has finished. In our day, during a celebration, if the wine or drinks were finished, the natural thing you would have thought of doing would be to go out and buy more drinks. But in this story, the reverse is the case. The wine has been finished, and the mother of our Lord Jesus Christ has come into the scene and told him (Jesus Christ) **"they have no wine"** (vs. 3). After hearing from Jesus she told the servants at the wedding **"whatsoever he saith unto you, do it."** (vs. 5)

Remember, Jesus Christ has not been well known during this period. The servants could have said, who is he that we have to do whatever he saith unto us, remember too he has not performed any miracle. They could have told Jesus mother you are out of your mind, or is he a magician? Also know the fact that it has not been recorded in the Bible where wine has finished in a wedding and somebody giving instructions to servants to do whatever they were told to do by another man. So there has never been a precedent of water being turned to wine.

Jesus told the servants to **"fill the water pots with water."** (vs.7) The servants could have left Jesus Christ standing there and walked away from him, saying the issue here was wine, with its own distinctive taste, and not water, for what comparison is there between water and wine?

The first act of obedience to Christ, even when it does not make sense to your natural senses, is demonstrated twice here. First the Bible recorded it in vs.7 **"and they filled them up (water pots) to the brim."** After this the Bible did not show or record that Jesus prayed, made signs, etc., but only said unto them in vs. 8 **"draw out now and bear unto the governor of the feast."**

The second act of the obedience of these servants was that seeing that Jesus Christ did not do anything to the water pots and asking them to bare it, they obeyed and bare it to the ruler of the feast and lo, the water tasted of wine.

Another significant part of this story is that the water Jesus turned into wine was the best of all the wine served at the feast, for the ruler said in vs.10 **"But thou hast kept the good wine until now."** The application is that after your obedience to Christ's promises and commandments, the best the Lord shall give you concerning his promises in your life.

Nevertheless as I am talking to you today as you are reading this book -- whatever the word of God asks you to do, do it. The servant twice obeyed Christ. This led to joy and satisfaction in this story. I pray that your obedience to Christ's commands will lead to joy and satisfaction in every area of your life (Amen).

9

Gideon's Army
(Judges 7)

"Then Jerubbaal, who is Gideon, and all the people that were with him, rose up early, and pitched beside the well of Harod: so that the host of the Midianites were on the north side of them, by the hill of Moreh, in the valley. And the LORD said unto Gideon, The people that are with thee are too many for me to give the Midianites into their hands, lest Israel vaunt themselves against me, saying, Mine own hand hath saved me. Now therefore go to, proclaim in the ears of the people, saying, Whosoever is fearful and afraid, let him return and depart early from mount Gilead. And there returned of the people twenty and two thousand; and there remained ten thousand. And the LORD said unto Gideon, The people are yet too many; bring them down unto the water, and I will try them for thee there: and it shall be, that of whom I say unto thee, This shall go with thee, the same shall go with thee; and of whomsoever I say unto thee, This shall not go with thee, the same shall not go. So he brought down the people unto the water: and the LORD said unto Gideon, Every one that lappeth of the water with his tongue, as a dog lappeth, him shalt thou set by himself; likewise every one that boweth down upon his knees to drink. And the number of them that lapped, putting their hand to their mouth, were three hundred men: but all the rest of the people bowed down upon their knees to drink water. And the LORD said unto Gideon, By the three hundred men that lapped will I save you, and deliver the Midianites into thine hand: and let all the other people go every man unto his place. So the people took victuals in their hand, and their trumpets: and he sent all the rest of Israel every man unto his tent, and retained those three hundred men: and the host of Midian was beneath him in the valley. And it came to pass the same night, that the LORD said unto him, Arise, get thee down unto the host; for I have delivered it into thine hand. But if thou fear to go down, go thou with Phurah thy servant down to the host: And thou shalt hear what they say; and afterward shall thine hands be strengthened to go down unto the host. Then went he down with Phurah his servant unto the outside of the armed men that were in the host. And the Midianites and the Amalekites and all the children of the east lay along in the valley like grasshoppers for multitude; and their camels were without number, as the sand by the sea side for multitude. And when Gideon was come, behold, there was a man that told a dream unto his fellow, and said, Behold, I dreamed a dream, and, lo, a cake of barley bread tumbled into the host of Midian, and came unto a tent, and smote it that it fell, and overturned it, that the tent lay along. And his fellow answered and said, This is nothing else save the sword of Gideon the son of Joash, a man of Israel: for into his hand hath God delivered Midian, and all the host. And it was so, when Gideon heard the telling of the dream, and the interpretation thereof, that he worshipped, and returned into the host of Israel, and said, Arise; for the LORD hath delivered into your hand the host of Midian. And he divided the three hundred men into three companies, and he put a trumpet in every man's hand, with empty pitchers, and lamps within the pitchers. And he said unto them, Look on me, and do likewise: and, behold, when I come to the outside of the camp, it shall be that, as I do, so shall ye do. When I blow with a trumpet, I and all that are with me, then blow ye the trumpets also on every side of all the camp, and say, The sword of the LORD, and of Gideon. So Gideon, and the hundred men that were with him, came unto the outside of the camp in the beginning of the middle watch; and they had but newly set the watch: and they blew the trumpets, and brake the pitchers that were in their hands. And the three companies blew the trumpets, and brake the pitchers, and held the lamps in their left hands, and the trumpets in their right hands to blow withal: and they cried, The sword of the LORD, and of Gideon. And they stood every man in his place round about the camp: and all the host ran, and cried, and fled. And the three hundred blew the trumpets, and the LORD set every man's sword against his fellow, even throughout all the host: and the host fled to Beth-shittah in Zererath, and to the border of Abel-meholah, unto Tabbath. And the men of Israel gathered themselves together out of Naphtali, and out of Asher, and out of all Manasseh, and pursued after the Midianites. And Gideon sent messengers throughout all mount Ephraim, saying, Come down against the Midianites, and take before them the waters unto Beth-barah and Jordan. Then all the men of Ephraim gathered themselves together, and took the waters unto Beth-barah and Jordan. And they took two princes of the Midianites, Oreb and Zeeb; and they slew Oreb upon the rock Oreb, and Zeeb they slew at the winepress of Zeeb, and pursued Midian, and

brought the heads of Oreb and Zeeb to Gideon on the other side Jordan." (Judges 7)

This is an account of God always at HIS very best. In a nutshell, the Israelites for their sin were being oppressed by the Midianites for good seven years (Judges 6) and God told Gideon that he would set them free from the hand of the Midianites with only 300 army men.

Who Are The Midianites?

The Midianites were Abraham's descendants through the union with one of his concubines by the name Keturah. **"Then again Abraham took a wife, and her name was Keturah. And she bare him Zimran, and Jokshan, and Medan, and Midian, and Ishbak, and Shuah"** (Genesis 25:1-2). So in a way they are related to the Israelites. Geographically, Midian was located in the Arabian land. The Midianites were the people that bought Joseph when his brothers sold him to slavery. In Genesis 37:23-36, bible says "and it came to pass, when Joseph was come unto his brethren, that they strip Joseph out of his coat, his coat of many colors that was on him; 24 And they took him, and cast him into a pit: and the pit was empty, there was no water in it.

25 And they sat down to eat bread: and they lifted up their eyes and looked, and, behold, a company of Ishmaelite came from Gilead with their camels bearing spicery and balm and myrrh, going to carry it down to Egypt. 26 And Judah said unto his brethren, what profit is it if we slay our brother, and conceal his blood? 27 Come, and let us sell him to the Ishmaelite, and let not our hand be upon him; for he is our brother and our flesh. And his brethren were

content. 28 Then there passed by Midianites merchantmen; and they drew and lifted up Joseph out of the pit, and sold Joseph to the Ishmaelite for twenty pieces of silver: and they brought Joseph into Egypt.

29 And Reuben returned unto the pit; and, behold, Joseph was not in the pit; and he rent his clothes. 30 And he returned unto his brethren, and said, the child is not; and I, whither shall I go? 31 And they took Joseph's coat, and killed a kid of the goats, and dipped the coat in the blood; 32 And they sent the coat of many colors, and they brought it to their father; and said, This have we found: know now whether it be thy son's coat or no. 33 And he knew it, and said, It is my son's coat; an evil beast hath devoured him; Joseph is without doubt rent in pieces. 34 And Jacob rent his clothes, and put sackcloth upon his loins, and mourned for his son many days. 35 And all his sons and all his daughters rose up to comfort him; but he refused to be comforted; and he said, for I will go down into the grave unto my son mourning. Thus his father wept for him. 36 And the Midianites sold him into Egypt unto Potiphar, an officer of Pharaoh's, and captain of the guard."

Also, out of fear of the Israelites, the Moabites and the Midianites conspired together to curse the Israelites.

"And the children of Israel set forward, and pitched in the plains of Moab on this side Jordan *by* Jericho.

And Balak the son of Zippor saw all that Israel had done to the Amorites. And Moab was sore afraid of the people, because they *were* many: and Moab was distressed because of the children of Israel. And Moab said unto the elders of

Mid'i-an, Now shall this company lick up all *that are* round about us, as the ox licketh up the grass of the field. And Balak the son of Zippor *was* king of the Moabites at that time.

He sent messengers therefore unto Ba'laam the son of Be'or to Pethor, which *is* by the river of the land of the children of his people, to call him, saying, Behold, there is a people come out from Egypt: Behold, they cover the face of the earth, and they abide over against me: come now therefore, I pray thee, curse me this people; for they *are* too mighty for me: peradventure I shall prevail, *that* we may smite them, and *that* I may drive them out of the land: for I wot that he whom thou blessest *is* blessed, and he whom thou cursest is cursed. And the elders of Moab and the elders of Mid'i-an departed with the rewards of divination in their hand; and they came unto Ba'laam, and spake unto him the words of Balak." (Numbers 22:1-7).

From all these accounts we can clearly see that there is a relationship with the Israelites that is not cordial, dating from ancient times. In the book of Judges this hostility still continues, as is evident as in Judges 6: 3-6 **"and so it was, when Israel had sown, that the Midianites came up, and the Amalekites, and the children of the east, even they came up against them; and they encamped against them, and destroyed the increase of the earth, till thou come unto Gaza, and left no sustenance for Israel, neither sheep, nor ox, nor ass. For they came up with their cattle and their tents, and they came as grasshoppers for multitude; for both they and their camels were without number; and they enter into the land to destroy it. And Israel was greatly impoverished because of the Midianites and the children of Israel cried unto the Lord."**

In short, the Midianites were harassing, burning and looting the Israelites that they nearly starved. With this background and oppression by the Midianites, the Israelites cried unto the Lord in Judges 6:7 **"And it came to pass, when the children of Israel cried unto the LORD because of the Midianites"** and the Lord in His infinite mercies raised up Gideon to be their leader who would deliver them from the oppression of the Midianites. After a leader was chosen for them after their crying out, God specifically told Gideon that he would liberate the Israelites from the oppression of the Midianites with only 300 soldiers. **DOES THIS MAKE SENSE TO YOUR NATURAL SENSES? NO IS THE ANSWER.** Considering the following facts viz:

- The Midianites and the Amalekites and all the children and all the children of the east were in multitude (large in number) as the sand by the seaside. Judges 7:12 **"And the Midianites and the Amalekites and all the children of the east lay along in the valley like grasshoppers for multitude; and their camels were without number, as the sand by the sea side for multitude."**
- The Midianites oppressed them for a solid seven years
- The Midianites oppression made Israel to live in fear, and by so doing were living in dens in the mountains and caves and strongholds
- They destroyed their crops and their animals, leading to…
- Impoverishment of the Israelites. Impoverishment means to make poor; to exhaust the strength or productivity

This is the state and condition the Israelites were living in when God told Gideon that He would deliver the Israelites from the hand of the Midianites with just 300 men **"…lest Israel vaunt themselves** against me, saying, mine own hand hath saved me" (Judges 7: 2). Glory belongs to God. In the book of Prophet Isaiah 42:8 God said **"I am the Lord: that is my name: and my glory will I not give to another, neither my praise to graven images."**

The Lord foreknew that if he allowed Gideon to go with all the strength of the army, they would praise themselves and not God. The account above is enough and provides plenty of strong reasons who anybody could advance to say: How can this war be won by only 300 men?

The first obedience of Gideon was found in Judges 7:3. **"Now therefore go to, proclaim in the ears of the people, saying, whosoever is fearful and afraid, let him return and depart early from mount Gilead, And there returned of the people twenty and two thousand; and there remained ten thousand."** He went and told the people as the Lord commanded.

The second obedience of Gideon was also recorded in Judges 7: 4-8. **"And the LORD said unto Gideon, The people are yet too many; bring them down unto the water, and I will try them for thee there: and it shall be, that of whom I say unto thee, This shall go with thee, the same shall go with thee; and of whomsoever I say unto thee, This shall not go with thee, the same shall not go. So he brought down the people unto the water: and the LORD said unto Gideon, Every one that lappeth of the water with his tongue, as a dog lappeth, him shalt thou set by himself; likewise every one that boweth down upon his knees to drink. And the number of them that lapped, putting their hand to their mouth, were three hundred men: but all the rest of the people bowed down upon their knees to drink water. And** the LORD said unto Gideon, By the three hundred men that lapped will I save you, and deliver the Midianites into thine hand: and let all the other people go every man unto his place. So the people took victuals in their hand, and their trumpets: and he sent all the rest of Israel every man unto his tent, and retained those three hundred men: and the host of Midian was beneath him in the valley."

He took the remaining ten thousand to the water and followed the instructions of the Lord and thereby 300 men were selected.

Another interesting point to know again is that it is after the obedience of Gideon to God has been fulfilled, that the Lord encouraged him to go with one of his servants by the name Phurah. Gideon went to war against the Midianites and the Lord gave victory to the Israelites. So children of God, obey the word of God even when it doesn't make sense to your natural senses. **Obedience first, then victory is assured.**

10

The Story of the Ten Healed Lepers
(Luke 17: 11-18)

"And it came to pass, as he went to Jerusalem that he passed through the midst of Samaria and Galilee. And as he entered into a certain village, there met him ten men that were lepers, which stood afar off: And they lifted up their voices, and said, Jesus, Master, have mercy on us. And when he saw them, he said unto them, Go show yourselves unto the priests. And it came to pass, that, as they went, they were cleansed. And one of them, when he saw that he was healed, turned back, and with a loud voice glorified God, And fell down on his face at his feet, giving him thanks: and he was a Samaritan. And Jesus answering said, Were there not ten cleansed? but where are the nine? There are not found that returned to give glory to God, save this stranger."

Before we can see the issue of obedience in this story, we need to refresh our memory regarding who the Samaritans are. What is the relationship between a Jew and a Samaritan? Where is Samaria?

Facts: They were people despised (I don't want to say hated) by the Jews. Why? The original settlers were the Jews, but were replaced when they were captured by King of Assyria because of the disobedience of the children of Israel. 2 Kings 17 verses 22-24 **"for the children of Israel walked in all the sins of Jeroboam which he did, they departed not from them, until the Lord removed Israel out of his sight, as he has said by all his servants the prophets. So was Israel carried away out of their own land to Assyria unto this day. And the King of Assyria brought men from Babylon, and from Cuthah and from Ava and from Hamath and from Sephaavaim, and placed them in the cities of Samaria instead of the children of Israel, and they possessed Samaria, and dwelt in the cities thereof"**

Where is Samaria? Bible says Samaria is the capital of the Northern Kingdom of Israel. The first occupant of the land of Samaria was king Omri who **"bought the hill of Samaria of Shemer for two talents of silver, and built on the hill, and called the name of the city which he bought, after the name of Shemer, owner of the hill of Samaria"** (I Kings 16:24).

We can conclude that the original settlers of the land of Samaria were the Israelites, but were later replaced by people sent their by the King of Assyria. This helps our understanding of this story, to know the relationship between Jews and the Samaritans when this miracle took place. In short, the "new" Samaritans were despised by the Jews. After the return of the captives of Israel during the time of Zerubbabel, they (the "new" Samaritans) made an effort to help to rebuild the temple, but their offer was turned down by the Israelites (Ezra 4: 2-3). When and after they were rejected, they started mocking the Jews, **"but it came to pass, that when Sanballat heard that we builded the wall, he was wroth, and took great indignation, and mocked the Jews. And he spoke** before his brethren and the army of Samaria, and said, what do these feeble Jews? Will they fortify themselves? Will they sacrifice? Will they make an end in a day? Will they revive the stones out of the heaps of the rubbish which are burned?" (Nehemiah 4:1-2).

Back to the story of ten lepers that were healed. We will look at the issue of obedience to Christ's command and thanksgiving. The ten lepers stood afar off because the custom was that they were usually isolated from the rest of the people. They knew who Jesus was. They knew he was the master. They knew he was and is still merciful. They knew he could change their situation. How did I know all these things? The Bible recorded in Luke 17:13 **"and they lifted up their voices, and said, Jesus, Master, have mercy on us."** Jesus responded to their cry by saying in Luke 17:14 **"Go show yourselves unto the priests."** The Bible says the lepers went to show themselves (Luke 17:14).

Look brethren in the Lord, this is what obedience to the Lord means even when it doesn't make sense to your natural senses. The Bible says as they went without questioning the Lord about why should they go and show themselves to the priests without following the rituals hand out in the cleansing of lepers in the book of Leviticus 14:1-32. Read the story of Naaman's Leprosy. One of the instructions is to sprinkle blood collected from one of the birds killed on the leper seven times after which he shall wash himself in water. This is the process law of healing lepers at that time. They (the ten lepers) could have said:

- Master, why don't you just speak the word and heal us right now?

- Master, isn't the priest supposed to kill birds so that their blood could be sprinkled on us 7 times (Leviticus 14:7)?
- Isn't the priest supposed to wash our clothes and shove off all our hairs (Leviticus 14:8)?
- Isn't the priest supposed to wash our flesh in water (Leviticus 14:9)?
- Isn't the priest supposed to offer sin offering, burnt offering, and meat offering upon the altar (Leviticus 14, 19-20)?
- Isn't the priest supposed to offer two turtle doves or two young pigeons, one for sin offering and the other a burnt offering (Leviticus 14:22)?

They could have asked one or two or all of these questions biblically and they would have been right in their own mind and senses. But the Bible recorded it that they went up and showed themselves unto the priest by simply obeying the word of GOD without asking all these possible questions, without any doubt, without discussion or entertaining fear. The Samaritans among them did not say, how can you heal me because the relationship between my people and your people is not cordial.

Brethren, it was their obedience to the Lord that healed them, even though the statement of our Lord Jesus Christ does not make sense to the natural senses, and it is different from the laws and rituals handed out in the book of Leviticus.

Out of these 10, only one returned to give thanks. That one happened to be a Samaritan who had a cultural wall difference. The only one who should have every reason to stay away was the one who came back and give thanks, and so received two things from the Lord: physical healing and spiritual healing, unlike the nine who got only physical healing. For God told the Samaritan, **"arise, go thy way: thy Faith hath made thee whole."** (Luke 17:19)

To apply this today, do you give thanks to the Lord after healing and miracles in your life? Do you just say it is my entitlement because I am a child of GOD? Thanksgiving is very important aspect of our Christian walk with GOD. Obey and give thanks.

11

Elisha Feeding a Hundred Men with Twenty Loaves
(2 Kings 4: 42:44)

"And there came a man from Baal-shalisha, and brought the man of God bread of the firstfruits, twenty loaves of barley, and full ears of corn in the husk thereof. And he said, Give unto the people, that they may eat. And his servitor said, What, should I set this before an hundred men? He said again, Give the people that they may eat: for thus saith the LORD, They shall eat, and shall leave thereof. So he set it before them, and they did eat, and left thereof, according to the word of the LORD." (2 Kings 4: 42-44)

Elisha had just restored back to life the dead son of a Shunamite woman, and he came to Gilgal where he met some group of people. (2 Kings 4:38). The principal focus here is the **"servitor"** of Elisha. His name was not recorded in the Bible, but we know he is male (vs. 44).

In this story, a man from the town of Baashali-sha brought 20 loaves of bread to Elisha. Elisha told his "servitor" to give the bread to people of hundred that they may eat. This is the point, to obey the word of GOD, spoken directly by GOD or through one of his prophets whether it makes sense or not to your natural senses. The attitude of the "servitor" is the same attitude that would be taken by any other natural person acting from his/her senses. In verse 43 of this chapter the "servitor" said **"what should I set this before on hundred men."** That sentence is a question more that a statement. This could mean that the "servitor" is telling Elisha that: don't you know that this is 20 loaves, how can these be sufficient for 100 grown up men. But the man of GOD (Elisha) told the "servitor" "give the people, that they may eat for thus saith the Lord, they shall eat, and shall leave thereof." The Bible says he set them (the 20 loaves) before the 100 men, they ate, and there was bread left over.

The story of the "servitor" could be likened to the way Moses reacted to GOD in the book of Numbers 11: 1-24 when GOD told him to gather the people so that he might give them flesh to eat. Moses told GOD that the men alone were 600,000 footmen (not counting the women and the children) -- how could this be possible? God told him to do what he asked him to do and he did even, though there was unbelief initially. Read the Book of Numbers Chapter 11:1-24. The "servitor" obeyed Elisha even though it doesn't make sense to him initially; it was his obedience to setting of the food before the 100 men that led to the miracle we are reading today. Your obedience to God's word through his/her servant will lead to miracles in your life today (Amen). Hear ye the word of God in 2 Chronicles 20:20 **"........Believe in the LORD your God, so shall ye be established; believe his prophets, so shall ye prosper."**

Breinigsville, PA USA
20 April 2010
236549BV00002B/41/P